I Got a Pet!

My Pet Rabbit

By Brienna Rossiter

www.littlebluehousebooks.com

Little Blue House is distributed by North Star Editions:
sales@northstareditions.com | 888-417-0195

Produced for Little Blue House by Red Line Editorial.

Photographs ©: Shutterstock Images, cover, 7, 8–9, 11, 15, 17, 18, 21 (top), 24 (top left), 24 (top right), 24 (bottom left), 24 (bottom right); iStockphoto, 4, 12, 21 (bottom), 23

Library of Congress Control Number: 2022901953

ISBN
978-1-64619-592-3 (hardcover)
978-1-64619-619-7 (paperback)
978-1-64619-671-5 (ebook pdf)
978-1-64619-646-3 (hosted ebook)

Printed in the United States of America
Mankato, MN
082022

About the Author

Brienna Rossiter is a writer and editor who lives in Minnesota.

Table of Contents

My Pet Rabbit **5**

Playtime **13**

Rabbit Care **19**

Glossary **24**

Index **24**

My Pet Rabbit

I have a pet rabbit.
She has long ears and
soft fur.

My rabbit lives in a cage.

The cage has shavings on the bottom.

They make the floor soft.

shavings

The cage has places where my rabbit can hide. Sometimes she sleeps there, too.

The cage has a litter box. My rabbit goes to the bathroom there.

litter box

Playtime

I can pick up my rabbit.

I take her out of the cage.

I hold and pet her.

Sometimes I let my rabbit play on the floor.
She runs and jumps.

Sometimes I take my rabbit outside.
She wears a harness and a leash.

leash
harness

brush

Rabbit Care

I take good care of my rabbit.

I brush her fur.

I feed my rabbit.
She eats pellets,
vegetables, and hay.

pellets
vegetable

I give my rabbit toys to chew. They keep her teeth healthy.

toy

Glossary

harness

shavings

pellets

vegetables

Index

B

brushing, 19

C

cage, 6, 8, 10, 13

F

feeding, 20

T

teeth, 22